Bramble Bear

The Missing Necklace

by Geoffrey Alan

illustrated by Pamela Storey

BRIMAX·NEWMARKET·ENGLAND

It is Bramble Bear's bedtime. He pulls on his pyjamas and slippers, then strolls into the sitting room.
"Goodnight," he says, yawning. But there is no reply. He sees his father sitting in a chair, his face hidden behind a big book.
" 'Detective Stories'," mutters Bramble, looking at the cover.

"Father, what does a detective do?" Bramble asks. His father puts down the book and answers. "He hunts for clues and solves mysteries."

"Wow!" says Bramble. "That sounds exciting. But is it hard?"

"Not always," grins his father. "I mean, I can see you have been in the cookie jar!"

Bramble gasps.

"How did you know?" asks Bramble.
"Because you have crumbs on your chin and pyjamas," chuckles his father.
"Mother did say I could have a cookie before I went to bed, as long as I brush my teeth," Bramble explains quickly.
"I wish I were a detective!"
That night, he dreams he is.

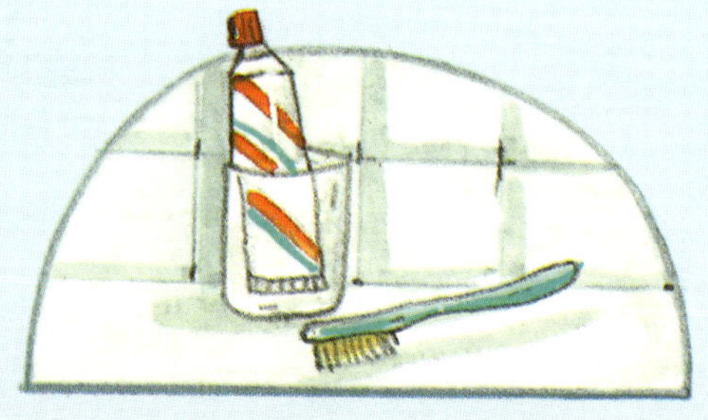

Next morning, when he wakes up, the sun is shining through his window.
Bramble dresses and hurries downstairs to see his father.
"He has gone out," says Bramble's mother.
"Can I borrow his magnifying glass?" asks Bramble. "The one he uses to look at his stamps."

"You must be very careful," Bramble's mother finally agrees. "Why do you want it?"

"Detectives always have them," says Bramble, "and that is what I am going to be!"

He sets off down the path but stops to peer through the magnifying glass at a spider. Bramble jumps. He forgets how big the special glass makes things seem!

"Now to search for clues," he thinks, walking on again. Suddenly, he sees some enormous, strange footprints. Bramble looks at them again, this time without his magnifying glass.

"They really are huge!" he mutters, in amazement. "Whatever could have made them? It's a mystery and I'm just the bear to solve it!"

Bramble thinks for a minute, then shivers.
"Perhaps it is a monster frog!"
Bravely, Bramble decides to find out. "That is what a real detective would do," he tells himself.
Bramble follows the tracks down to the river. They lead right into the water.

Bramble tiptoes on to the old wooden bridge.
“If it is a monster frog, I will soon see. I shall just wait here quietly,” he thinks.
But no sooner does he glance down at the river, than lots of bubbles rise to the surface.
Bramble hears an odd gurgling sound below him.

Next moment, a figure appears. Poor Bramble is so surprised, he steps back and stumbles.
Only then does he notice something sparkle in the sunlight. Before he can look closer, he hears his father call, "Are you all right?"
"I think so," Bramble replies, sitting up. "I thought you were a monster frog!"

"Hardly!" laughs his father. "But I have been diving." He climbs up on to the riverbank and pulls off his goggles. Bramble sees he is wearing flippers.

"So they made those strange tracks," he frowns.

"Your mother lost her necklace here," explains his father.

Bramble gasps. "That must be what I saw shining!"

"Here it is!" cries Bramble. "Mother's necklace didn't fall in the water. Look! It's hooked on to the bottom of the bridge!"

"Well done, son," chuckles Bramble's father. "However did you know?"

"Oh, clues, I suppose," begins Bramble. Then he grins, "Or just good luck, really."

"What a clever detective you are!" smiles Bramble's mother, when he gives her the necklace. She puts it on, straight away. "I hope you did not mind me using your magnifying glass?" says Bramble to his father. "You can keep it," replies his father. "A detective always needs one!"

"That is very kind of you, Dad," says Bramble. "But I don't think I want to be a detective any more."

"Why ever not?" asks Bramble's father as Bramble gives him back the magnifying glass.

"Well," begins Bramble, shuffling his feet, "if I had seen a monster frog, I would have been really frightened!"

Say these words again

hidden
clues
crumbs
borrow
teeth
goggles
monster

bubbles
sparkle
flippers
wait
detective
cookie
stumble